The Best Belgian Waffle Cookbook

Tons of Amazing Recipes to Make the
Perfect Belgian Waffles

Table of Contents

Introduction

Time to wake up and smell the waffles! Belgian waffles are a great breakfast tradition and now you are equipped with so many recipes to make as many as you'd like. From classic, yeast-raised waffles to our recipe for extra-fluffy waffles, there are several foundational recipes that you must try. These 'basic' recipes are super easy to make and can be topped with almost anything – a drizzle of traditional maple syrup will do too! Once you have mastered the basic Belgian waffle, it's time to explore the rest of this recipe book and prepare to be surprised and delighted with some of the newer waffle recipes you might not have thought of!

I decided to write this book when I realized how much I absolutely love waffles. I could eat them for breakfast, lunch, and dinner! My Belgian waffle maker is always sitting on the counter in my kitchen as there is no need to put it away; I use it all the time! I wanted to share some of my recipes for Belgian waffles that you might not have thought to try. For example, the recipe for Cinnamon-Roll Belgian Waffles is so easy yet mind-blowingly delicious – why didn't anyone make these Belgian waffles sooner?! Mozzarella-Stick Waffles are another fantastic way to use your Belgian Waffle maker. Try the Cheddar Waffle recipe and use the Belgian waffles as 'bread' for any sandwich. You will never look at your Belgian waffle iron the same. So, plug in your waffle maker, open up this recipe book, and make some tasty waffles. They will be a hit any time of the day!

Pumpkin Pecan Waffles

This recipe is like a combination of pumpkin pie and pecan pie all nicely put together in a beautiful Belgian waffle. While these waffles taste so much like fall, enjoy them anytime of the year!

Yield: 8 Servings

Active Time: 15 minutes

Ingredients:

- 3/4 cup pecans
- 1/2 cup coconut oil
- 1/2 cup brown sugar
- 1/4 cup white sugar
- 1 1/2 cups pumpkin puree
- 2 separated eggs
- 1/2 cup whole milk
- 3 teaspoons vanilla extract
- 1 1/2 Tablespoons pumpkin spice
- 1 1/2 cups flour
- 3 teaspoons baking powder
- 1/2 teaspoon salt

Directions:

1. Using a hand blender, whip the egg whites to medium soft peaks. Then, set aside for now

2. In a large bowl, mix the coconut oil, milk, sugars, pumpkin puree, and yolks. Whisk until smooth.

3. Add the pumpkin spice and vanilla extract to the bowl with the pumpkin and mix together.

4. Add the dry ingredients to the bowl and whisk until smooth.

5. Gently add the egg whites into the batter. Mix until combined but don't beat the batter too hard- you want it to stay nice and fluffy

6. Chop the pecans and then fold into the batter

7. Preheat your waffle iron then pour the batter in and close to cook.

8. Once the waffles are done, remove from the waffle iron and serve!

Pumpkin Waffles

Get ready for some delicious, fluffy pumpkin waffles. By whipping the egg whites separate from the yolks, these waffles turn out incredibly light and so full of delicious fall flavors.

Yield: 8 Servings

Active Time: 15 minutes

Ingredients:

- 1/2 cup coconut oil
- 1/2 cup brown sugar
- 1/4 cup white sugar
- 1 1/2 cups pumpkin puree
- 2 separated eggs
- 1/2 cup whole milk
- 3 teaspoons vanilla extract
- 1 1/2 Tablespoons pumpkin spice
- 1 1/2 cups flour
- 3 teaspoons baking powder

1/2 teaspoon salt

Directions:

1. Using a hand blender, whip the egg whites to medium soft peaks. Then, set aside for now

2. In a large bowl, mix the coconut oil, milk, sugars, pumpkin puree, and yolks. Whisk until smooth.

3. Add the pumpkin spice and vanilla extract to the bowl with the pumpkin and mix together.

4. Add the dry ingredients to the bowl and whisk until smooth.

5. Gently add the egg whites into the batter. Mix until combined but don't beat the batter too hard- you want it to stay nice and fluffy

6. Preheat your waffle iron then pour the batter in and close to cook.

7. Once the waffles are done, remove from the waffle iron and serve!

Classic Belgian Waffles

If you love traditional Belgian waffles, then here is the perfect recipe for you. Easy to put together and delicious every time, you really can't go wrong with this recipe.

Yield: 8 servings

Active Time: 15 minutes

Ingredients:

- 2 cups flour
- 1 tablespoon of baking powder
- 4 tablespoons granulated sugar
- 1 teaspoons salt
- 2 eggs, lightly whisked
- 1 1/2 cups milk

- 1/3 cup vegetable oil
- 1 teaspoon vanilla extract

Directions:

1. In a medium bowl, whisk all the dry ingredients (flour, baking powder, sugar, and salt) together.

2. In a separate, small bowl, whisk all the wet ingredients (the milk, eggs, vegetable oil and vanilla) together.

3. Slowly put all the wet ingredients into the dry, whisking constantly until smooth and lump-free. (If you do have any lumps, use a rubber spatula to press them against the side of the bowl and break them up.)

4. Heat your waffle maker according to your manufacturer's directions.

5. Cook the batter according to your waffle maker's directions – every machine is slightly different regarding cooking time! Enjoy these waffles while they are still hot, paired with your favorite toppings.

Yeast-Raised Belgian Waffles

Crispy on the outside and chewy on the inside, these Belgian waffles have a great texture and flavor. Leavening the waffles with yeast is a traditional method that is sure to taste great!

Active Time: 15 minutes

Yield: 5 servings

Ingredients:

- 1 1/2 cups warm milk
- 1 1/2 teaspoons dry instant yeast
- 5 tablespoons of melted butter
- 1 tablespoon sugar
- 2 teaspoons vanilla extract
- 2 eggs
- 2 cups flour
- 1/2 teaspoons salt

Directions:

1. In a medium bowl, mix the yeast, milk, and sugar together. Set aside for about 5 minutes, until the yeast begins to grow and the mixture looks frothy.

2. Add the remaining ingredients to the bowl and whisk together. (Don't worry about any lumps just yet.)

3. Cover the bowl and let the batter sit for about an hour. At this point, you can also cover the bowl and refrigerate the batter for the next day – it will stay good for about 24 hours if refrigerated.

4. Heat your waffle iron and cook the batter according to the manufacturer's directions.

5. Serve the waffles while hot!

Extra-Fluffy Belgian Waffles

If you like your waffles super fluffy, then this is the recipe for you. Whipping the egg whites separately from the yolks and folding them into the batter makes these waffles so light and tasty.

Yield: 6 servings

Active Time: 15 minutes

Ingredients:

- 2 cups flour
- 1 tablespoon of baking powder
- 4 tablespoons granulated sugar
- 1 teaspoons salt

- 2 eggs separated
- 1 1/2 cups milk
- 1/3 cup vegetable oil
- 1 teaspoon vanilla extract

Directions:

1. In a medium sized bowl, whisk the egg whites until they form soft peaks. Set aside.

2. In a separate, medium bowl, whisk all of dry ingredients (flour, baking powder, sugar, and salt) together.

3. In another small bowl, whisk all the wet ingredients (the milk, vegetable oil, egg yolks, and vanilla) together.

4. Slowly add the wet ingredients to the dry, whisking constantly until smooth and lump-free. (If you do have any lumps, use a rubber spatula to press them against the side of the bowl and break them up.)

5. Gently fold the whipped egg whites into the batter until fully combined.

6. Heat your waffle maker and cook the batter according to your manufacturer's directions – every machine is slightly different regarding time.

7. Enjoy these waffles while they are still hot, alone or paired with your favorite toppings.

Maple-Bacon Waffles

Bacon pieces and delicious maple syrup are combined in this delicious waffle. It truly is a whole breakfast in one waffle!

Yield: 8 servings

Active Time: 15 minutes

Ingredients:

- 2 cups flour
- 1 tablespoon of baking powder
- 3 tablespoons maple syrup
- 1 teaspoons salt
- 2 eggs, lightly whisked
- 1 1/2 cups milk
- 1/3 cup vegetable oil

- 1 teaspoon vanilla extract
- 1/2 cup cooked, crumbled bacon

Directions:

1. In a medium bowl, whisk all the dry ingredients (flour, baking powder, and salt) together.

2. In a separate, small bowl, whisk all the wet ingredients (the milk, vegetable oil, maple syrup, eggs, and vanilla) together.

3. Slowly add the wet ingredients to the dry, whisking constantly until smooth and lump-free. (If you do have any lumps, use a rubber spatula to press them against the side of the bowl and break them up.)

4. Mix in the crumbled bacon pieces.

5. Heat your waffle maker according to your manufacturer's directions. Even if you have a non-stick waffle maker, we recommend using cooking spray to ensure that the bacon pieces do not stick.

6. Cook the batter according to your waffle maker's directions – every machine is slightly different regarding cooking time! Enjoy these waffles while they are still hot, alone or with some extra maple syrup on top!

Apple-Cinnamon Waffles

With apples baked right into the waffle, these are sure to be a hit. This recipe makes delicious waffles that taste just like apple pie for breakfast!

Yield: 8 servings

Active Time: 15 minutes

Ingredients:

- 2 1/ 4 cups flour
- 1 tablespoon of baking powder

- 4 tablespoons granulated sugar
- 1 tablespoon cinnamon
- 1 teaspoons salt
- 2 eggs, lightly whisked
- 3/4 cups milk
- 1/3 cup vegetable oil
- 1 teaspoon vanilla extract
- 1/2 cup grated apples

Directions:

1. In a medium bowl, whisk all the dry ingredients (flour, baking powder, cinnamon, sugar, and salt) together.

2. In a separate, small bowl, whisk all the wet ingredients (the milk, eggs, vegetable oil and vanilla) together.

3. Slowly put the wet ingredients into the dry, whisking constantly until smooth and lump-free. (If you do have any lumps, use a rubber spatula to press them against the side of the bowl and break them up.)

4. Fold in the grated apples.

5. Heat your waffle maker according to your manufacturer's directions.

6. Cook the batter according to your waffle maker's directions – every machine is slightly different regarding cooking time! Enjoy these waffles while they are still hot, alone or paired with your favorite toppings.

Peanut-Butter Belgian Waffles

A super hearty waffle that adds some great flavor and protein to your breakfast. Top these waffles with some jelly and you'll have a new twist on a PB&J!

Yield: 8 servings

Active Time: 15 minutes

Ingredients:

- 1 3/4 cups flour
- 1 tablespoon of baking powder
- 4 tablespoons granulated sugar
- 1 teaspoons salt
- 2 eggs, lightly whisked
- 1 1/2 cups milk
- 1/4 cup vegetable oil

- 1 teaspoon vanilla extract
- 1/4 cup peanut butter

Directions:

1. In a medium bowl, whisk all of the dry ingredients (flour, baking powder, sugar, and salt) together.

2. In a separate, small bowl, whisk all of the wet ingredients (the milk, eggs, vegetable oil, and vanilla) together.

3. In another bowl, add about 1/4 of the wet mixture and the peanut butter and whisk until the peanut butter is smooth. Add the remaining wet ingredients and whisk constantly to ensure the peanut butter is fully combined and doesn't clump.

4. Slowly add the wet ingredients to the dry, whisking constantly until smooth and limp-free. (If you do have any lumps, use a rubber spatula to press them against the side of the bowl and break them up.)

5. Heat your waffle maker and cook the batter according to your manufacturer's directions.

6. Enjoy these waffles while they are still hot, alone or paired with your favorite toppings.

Peanut Butter and Banana Belgian Waffles

This recipe makes a decadent banana cake with a hearty peanut butter flavor. This is a perfect way to use over-ripe bananas that you may have around the house – the riper the better!

Yield: 8 servings

Active Time: 15 minutes

Ingredients:

- 1 3/4 cups flour
- 1 tablespoon of baking powder
- 4 tablespoons granulated sugar
- 1 teaspoons salt
- 2 eggs, lightly whisked
- 1 1/2 cups milk
- 1/4 cup vegetable oil
- 1 teaspoon vanilla extract
- 1/4 cup peanut butter
- 1 large ripe banana

Directions:

1. In a medium bowl, whisk all the dry ingredients (flour, baking powder, sugar, and salt) together.

2. In a separate, small bowl, whisk all the wet ingredients (the milk, eggs, vegetable oil, and vanilla) together.

3. In another bowl, add about 1/4 of the wet mixture and the peanut butter and whisk until the peanut butter is smooth. Add the remaining wet ingredients and whisk constantly to ensure the peanut butter if fully combined and doesn't clump.

4. Mash the ripe banana into the peanut butter mixture.

5. Slowly add the wet ingredients to the dry, whisking constantly until smooth and lump-free. (If you do have any lumps, use a rubber spatula to press them against the side of the bowl and break them up.)

6. Heat your waffle maker and cook the batter according to your manufacturer's directions.

7. Enjoy these waffles while they are still hot, alone or paired with your favorite toppings.

Gluten-Free Belgian Waffles

Perfect Belgian waffles made gluten-free! Anyone with gluten restrictions will love these waffles.

Yield: 8 servings

Active Time: 10 minutes

Ingredients:

- 2 cups gluten-free, all-purpose flour
- 1 tablespoon of baking powder
- 4 tablespoons granulated sugar
- 1 teaspoons salt
- 2 eggs, lightly whisked
- 1 1/2 cups milk
- 1/3 cup vegetable oil
- 1 teaspoon vanilla extract

Directions:

1. In a medium bowl, whisk all the dry ingredients (gluten free flour, baking powder, sugar, and salt) together.

2. In a separate, small bowl, whisk all of the wet ingredients (the milk, eggs, vegetable oil, and vanilla) together.

3. Slowly add the wet ingredients to the dry, whisking constantly until smooth and lump-free. (If you do have any lumps, use a rubber spatula to press them against the side of the bowl and break them up.)

4. Heat your waffle maker and cook the batter according to your manufacturer's directions.

5. Enjoy these waffles while they are still hot, alone or paired with your favorite toppings.

Toasted Coconut Belgian Waffles

Full of tropical coconut flavor, these waffles are amazing in the summertime! No need to toast the coconut before adding it to the batter, the waffle iron will take care of that for you.

Yield: 8 servings

Active Time: 15 minutes

Ingredients:

- 2 cups flour
- 1 tablespoon of baking powder
- 4 tablespoons granulated sugar
- 1 teaspoons salt
- 2 eggs, lightly whisked
- 1 1/2 cups milk
- 1/3 cup vegetable oil
- 1 teaspoon vanilla extract
- 1/2 cup sweetened, shredded coconut

Directions:

1. In a medium bowl, whisk all the dry ingredients (flour, baking powder, sugar, coconut flakes, and salt) together.

2. In a separate, small bowl, whisk all the wet ingredients (the milk, eggs, vegetable oil, and vanilla) together.

3. Slowly add the wet ingredients to the dry, whisking constantly until smooth and lump-free. (If you do have any lumps, use a rubber spatula to press them against the side of the bowl and break them up.)

4. Heat your waffle maker and cook the batter according to your manufacturer's directions.

5. Enjoy these waffles while they are still hot, alone or paired with your favorite toppings.

Piña Colada Belgian Waffles

All of the delicious flavors of a piña colada put together in a waffle. The super easy pineapple topping makes these waffles irresistible!

Yield: 8 servings

Active Time: 15 minutes

Ingredients:

- 2 cups flour
- 1 tablespoon of baking powder
- 4 tablespoons granulated sugar
- 1 teaspoons salt
- 2 eggs, lightly whisked
- 1 1/2 cups milk
- 1/3 cup vegetable oil
- 2 teaspoons run extract
- 1/2 cup shredded, sweetened coconut
- 1 can crushed pineapple
- 2 tablespoons sugar

Directions:

1. In a medium bowl, whisk all the dry ingredients (flour, baking powder, sugar, coconut flakes, and salt) together.

2. In a separate, small bowl, whisk all the wet ingredients together (the milk, eggs, vegetable oil, and rum extract) together.

3. Slowly add the wet ingredients to the dry, whisking constantly until smooth and lump-free. (If you do have any lumps, use a rubber spatula to press them against the side of the bowl and break them up.)

4. Heat your waffle maker and cook the batter according to your manufacturer's directions.

5. In a small saucepan, bring the crushed pineapple (with the juice from the can) and the sugar to a boil, boiling until the liquid thickens.

6. Top the Belgian waffles with the crushed pineapple topping and enjoy!

Cheddar Waffles

These waffles are a great savory treat that works well for lunch or dinner. Try a sweet and salty combination by topping these with vanilla ice cream, or use two waffles as the 'bread' for a sandwich.

Yield: 8 servings

Active Time: 15 minutes

Ingredients:

- 2 cups flour
- 1 tablespoon of baking powder
- 4 tablespoons granulated sugar
- 1 teaspoons salt
- 1 teaspoon black pepper

- 2 eggs, lightly whisked
- 1 1/2 cups milk
- 1/3 cup vegetable oil
- 1/2 cup shredded cheddar cheese

Directions:

1. In a medium bowl, whisk all the dry ingredients (flour, baking powder, sugar, pepper, cheddar cheese, and salt) together.

2. In a separate, small bowl, whisk all of the wet ingredients (the milk, vegetable oil, and eggs) together.

3. Slowly add the wet ingredients to the dry, whisking constantly until smooth and lump-free. (If you do have any lumps, use a rubber spatula to press them against the side of the bowl and break them up.)

4. Heat your waffle maker according to your manufacturer's directions. Even if you have a non-stick waffle maker, we recommend using cooking spray to prevent the cheese from sticking to the machine as it melts

5. Cook the batter according to your waffle maker's directions – every machine is slightly different regarding cooking time!

Apple Cheddar Waffles

If you love cheddar cheese on apple pie, then these waffles are perfect for you. The perfect combination of sweet and salty, these waffles are great anytime of the day – so don't put that waffle maker away after breakfast!

Yield: 8 servings

Active Time: 20 minutes

Ingredients:

- 2 cups flour
- 1 tablespoon of baking powder
- 4 tablespoons granulated sugar
- 1 teaspoons salt
- 2 eggs, lightly whisked

- 1 cup milk
- 1/3 cup vegetable oil
- 1/2 cup shredded cheddar cheese
- 1/2 cup grated apples

Directions:

1. In a medium bowl, whisk all of the dry ingredients (flour, baking powder, sugar, pepper, cheddar cheese, and salt) together.

2. In a separate, small bowl, whisk all the wet ingredients (the milk, vegetable oil, grated apples, and eggs) together.

3. Slowly add the wet ingredients to the dry, whisking constantly until smooth and lump-free. (If you do have any lumps, use a rubber spatula to press them against the side of the bowl and break them up.)

4. Heat your waffle maker according to your manufacturer's directions. Even if you have a non-stick waffle maker, we recommend using cooking spray to prevent the cheese from sticking to the machine as it melts

5. Cook the batter according to your waffle maker's directions – every machine is slightly different regarding cooking time!

Carrot-Cake Belgian Waffles

Carrot cake for breakfast? It's possible when you make this waffle recipe! Top these delicious waffles with maple syrup, whipped cream, or even a cream cheese frosting for a decadent breakfast.

Yield: 8 servings

Active Time: 20 minutes

Ingredients:

- 2 cups flour
- 1 tablespoon of baking powder
- 4 tablespoons granulated sugar

- 1 teaspoon cinnamon
- 1/4 teaspoon nutmeg
- 1 teaspoons salt
- 2 eggs, lightly whisked
- 1 1cups milk
- 1/3 cup vegetable oil
- 2 teaspoon vanilla extract
- 1/2 cup grated carrots

Directions:

1. In a medium bowl, whisk all the dry ingredients (flour, baking powder, sugar, cinnamon, nutmeg, and salt) together.

2. In a separate, small bowl, whisk all the wet ingredients (the milk, eggs, vegetable oil, and vanilla) together.

3. Slowly add the wet ingredients to the dry, whisking constantly until smooth and lump-free. (If you do have any lumps, use a rubber spatula to press them against the side of the bowl and break them up.)

4. Add the grated carrots to the batter and mix well.

5. Heat your waffle maker and cook the batter according to your manufacturer's directions.

Cinnamon-Roll Belgian Waffles

Why hasn't anyone made these cinnamon roll waffles sooner?! No more waiting for cinnamon rolls to bake; these cinnamon-roll waffles only take about two minutes and, voilà, it's time to eat!

Yield: 6 servings

Active Time: 5 minutes

Ingredients:

- 1 can of store bought cinnamon rolls (un-cooked, found in the refrigerated section of the store)

Directions:

1. Open the can of cinnamon-roll dough and remove the pre-shaped cinnamon rolls.

2. Heat your waffle iron according to the manufacturer's directions.

3. Place one cinnamon roll in the middle of the waffle iron square.

4. Close the waffle iron and cook as you would a normal waffle.

5. Once the cinnamon rolls are cooked, spread the frosting that came with the cinnamon rolls on top.

Chive Belgian Waffles with Crème Fraiche

This waffle makes me think of being at a fancy brunch. A savory waffle batter is topped with a simple crème fraiche which is not only delicious but make you feel very grown up!

Yield: 8 servings

Active Time: 15 minutes

Ingredients:

- 2 cups flour
- 1 tablespoon of baking powder
- 2 tablespoons granulated sugar
- 1/2 teaspoon black pepper
- 1 teaspoons salt
- 2 eggs, lightly whisked
- 1 1/2 cups milk
- 1/3 cup vegetable oil
- 1/4 cup chopped chives
- 1/2 cup crème fraiche

Directions:

1. In a medium bowl, whisk all of the dry ingredients (flour, baking powder, sugar, pepper, chives, and salt) together.

2. In a separate, small bowl, whisk the wet ingredients, excluding the crème fraiche (the milk, vegetable oil, and eggs) together.

3. Slowly add the wet ingredients to the dry, whisking constantly until smooth and lump-free. (If you do have any lumps, use a rubber spatula to press them against the side of the bowl and break them up.)

4. Heat your waffle maker and cook the batter according to your manufacturer's directions.

5. Place a scoop of crème fraiche on top of the waffle right before serving.

Fun-fetti Waffles

Fun-fetti cake meets waffles in this easy to make recipe. Perfect for a birthday breakfast or anytime you need some festive sprinkles in your life!

Yield: 8 servings

Active Time: 10 minutes

Ingredients:

- 2 cups flour
- 1 tablespoon of baking powder

- 4 tablespoons granulated sugar
- 1 teaspoons salt
- 2 eggs, lightly whisked
- 1 1/2 cups milk
- 1/3 cup vegetable oil
- 1 teaspoon vanilla extract
- 1/4 cup rainbow sprinkles

Directions:

1. In a medium bowl, whisk all of the dry ingredients (flour, baking powder, sugar, sprinkles, and salt) together.

2. In a separate, small bowl, whisk all of the wet ingredients (the milk, eggs, vegetable oil, and vanilla) together.

3. Slowly add the wet ingredients to the dry, whisking constantly until smooth and lump-free. (If you do have any lumps, use a rubber spatula to press them against the side of the bowl and break them up.)

4. Heat your waffle maker according to your manufacturer's directions. I recommend using a cooking spray for these waffles even if you waffle maker is non-stick.

5. Cook the batter according to your waffle maker's directions. Enjoy these waffles while they are still hot, alone or paired with your favorite toppings.

Chocolate Waffles

These waffles, full of rich cocoa powder, just made breakfast time even better! Top these waffles with chocolate syrup and whipped cream for a waffle that is similar to a sundae.

Yield: 8 servings

Active Time: 15 minutes

Ingredients:

- 1 3/4 cups flour
- 1 tablespoon of baking powder
- 1/4 cup cocoa powder
- 5 tablespoons granulated sugar
- 1 teaspoons salt
- 2 eggs, lightly whisked
- 1 1/2 cups milk
- 1/3 cup vegetable oil
- 2 teaspoon vanilla extract

Directions:

1. In a medium bowl, whisk all of the dry ingredients (flour, baking powder, sugar, cocoa powder, and salt) together.

2. In a separate, small bowl, whisk all of the wet ingredients (the milk, eggs, vegetable oil, and vanilla) together.

3. Slowly add the wet ingredients to the dry, whisking constantly until smooth and lump-free. (If you do have any lumps, use a rubber spatula to press them against the side of the bowl and break them up.)

4. Heat your waffle maker and cook the batter according to your manufacturer's directions.

5. Enjoy these waffles while they are still hot, alone or paired with your favorite toppings (chocolate sauce and whipped cream are a great place to start!).

Chocolate, Peanut-Butter Waffles

The chocolate and peanut butter combination is hard to resist and these waffles will be too! The chopped Reese's peanut-butter cups are just the icing on the cake – or the perfect topping on the waffle!

Yield: 8 servings

Active Time: 15 minutes

Ingredients:

- 1 3/4 cups flour
- 1 tablespoon of baking powder
- 1/4 cup cocoa powder
- 5 tablespoons granulated sugar
- 1 teaspoons salt

- 2 eggs, lightly whisked
- 1/4 cup peanut butter
- 1 1/2 cups milk
- 1/4 cup vegetable oil
- 2 teaspoon vanilla extract
- 1/2 cup chopped Reese's peanut butter cups

Directions:

1. In a medium bowl, whisk all of the dry ingredients (flour, baking powder, sugar, cocoa powder, and salt) together.

2. In a separate, small bowl, whisk all of the wet ingredients (the milk, eggs, vegetable oil, and vanilla) together.

3. In another bowl add about 1/4 of the wet mixture and the peanut butter and whisk until the peanut butter is smooth. Add the remaining wet ingredients, whisking constantly to ensure the peanut butter if fully combined and doesn't clump.

4. Slowly add the wet ingredients to the dry, whisking constantly until smooth and lump-free. (If you do have any lumps, use a rubber spatula to press them against the side of the bowl and break them up.)

5. Heat your waffle maker and cook the batter according to your manufacturer's directions.

6. Top with chopped peanut butter cups and serve while hot.

Lemon-Meringue Belgian Waffles

Lemon curd and marshmallow fluff make this waffle look and taste like a lemon meringue pie. Pie for breakfast? Yes, please!

Yield: 6 servings

Active Time: 15 minutes

Ingredients:

- 2 cups flour
- 1 tablespoon of baking powder
- 4 tablespoons granulated sugar
- 1 teaspoons salt
- 2 eggs separated
- 1 1/2 cups milk
- 1/3 cup vegetable oil
- 1 teaspoon vanilla extract
- 3/4 cup lemon curd
- 1/2 cup marshmallow fluff

Directions:

1. In a medium bowl, whisk the egg whites until they form soft peaks. Set aside.

2. In a separate, medium bowl, whisk all of the dry ingredients (flour, baking powder, sugar, and salt) together.

3. In another, small bowl, whisk all of the wet ingredients (the milk, vegetable oil, egg yolks, and vanilla) together.

4. Slowly add the wet ingredients to the dry, whisking constantly until smooth and lump-free. (If you do have any lumps, use a rubber spatula to press them against the side of the bowl and break them up.)

5. Gently fold the whipped egg whites into the batter until fully combined.

6. Heat your waffle maker and cook the batter according to your manufacturer's directions.

7. Spread a layer of lemon curd on each waffle and top it with the marshmallow fluff.

8. Torch the marshmallow fluff with a kitchen blow torch to slightly brown the fluff.

9. Serve while hot!

Chocolate-Chip Chocolate Waffles

Warm, melty chocolate chips are baking into these chocolate waffles making a chocolate lover's dream breakfast a reality! Serve them hot to ensure that the chocolate chips stay soft and gooey.

Yield: 8 servings

Active Time: 15 minutes

Ingredients:

- 1 3/4 cups flour
- 1 tablespoon of baking powder
- 1/4 cup cocoa powder
- 5 tablespoons granulated sugar
- 1 teaspoons salt
- 2 eggs, lightly whisked

- 1 1/2 cups milk
- 1/3 cup vegetable oil
- 2 teaspoon vanilla extract
- 1/2 cup mini chocolate chips

Directions:

1. In a medium bowl, whisk all of dry ingredients (flour, baking powder, sugar, cocoa powder, mini chocolate chips, and salt) together.

2. In a separate, small bowl, whisk all of the wet ingredients (the milk, eggs, vegetable oil, and vanilla) together.

3. Slowly add the wet ingredients to the dry, whisking constantly until smooth and lump-free. (If you do have any lumps, use a rubber spatula to press them against the side of the bowl and break them up.)

4. Heat your waffle maker and cook the batter according to your manufacturer's directions.

5. Enjoy these waffles while they are still hot, alone or paired with your favorite toppings (chocolate sauce and whipped cream are a great place to start!).

Belgian Waffle BLT

A savory waffle is made into the bread of this BLT sandwich. No more using boring old bread – fresh waffles are the way to go!

Yield: 4 sandwiches

Active Time: 15 minutes

Ingredients:

- 2 cups flour
- 1 tablespoon of baking powder
- 2 tablespoons granulated sugar
- 1 teaspoons salt
- 1/2 teaspoon black pepper
- 2 eggs, lightly whisked
- 1 1/2 cups milk
- 1/3 cup vegetable oil
- 1 medium tomato, sliced
- 8 iceberg lettuce leaves
- 8 slices of bacon
- 1/2 cup mayonnaise

Directions:

1. In a medium bowl, whisk all of the dry ingredients (flour, baking powder, sugar, pepper, and salt) together.

2. In a separate, small bowl, whisk all of the wet ingredients (the milk, vegetable oil, and eggs) together.

3. Slowly add the wet ingredients to the dry, whisking constantly until smooth and lump-free. (If you do have any lumps, use a rubber spatula to press them against the side of the bowl and break them up.)

4. Heat your waffle maker and cook the batter according to your manufacturer's directions.

5. Divide the mayonnaise between four of the waffles and spread it around to cover the whole waffle.

6. Place two of the lettuce leave on top followed by two slices of bacon and two slices of tomato.

7. Top the sandwich with another Belgian waffle and eat!

Belgian-Waffle Mozzarella Sticks

No need to fry these mozzarella sticks, they will cook perfectly in your waffle maker. Serve with a side of marinara sauce for a super delicious appetizer or snack.

Yield: 8 servings

Active Time: 20 minutes

Ingredients:

- 2 cups flour
- 1 tablespoon of baking powder
- 2 tablespoons granulated sugar
- 1/2 teaspoon black pepper
- 1/2 teaspoon dried basil
- 1 teaspoons salt
- 2 eggs, lightly whisked

- 1 1/2 cups milk
- 1/3 cup vegetable oil
- 3/4 cup grated mozzarella

Directions:

1. In a medium bowl, whisk all of the dry ingredients (flour, baking powder, sugar, and salt) together.

2. In a separate, small bowl, whisk all of the wet ingredients (the milk, eggs, vegetable oil, and vanilla) together.

3. Slowly add the wet ingredients to the dry, whisking constantly until smooth and lump-free. (If you do have any lumps, use a rubber spatula to press them against the side of the bowl and break them up.)

4. Heat your waffle maker according to your manufacturer's directions.

5. Pour about 1/2 cup of waffle batter into the waffle iron, spreading it out evenly.

6. Sprinkle about 1/8 cup of mozzarella cheese on top of the batter and pour about 1/4 more batter on top.

7. Close the waffle iron and cook the batter according to your waffle makers direction's.

8. Cut the Belgian waffle into strips and serve while hot!

Maple-Bourbon Belgian Waffles

Of course, maple syrup goes with waffles, but bourbon? Absolutely! Maple and bourbon flavors fill these waffles making them a tasty breakfast or a base for a dessert. The alcohol from the bourbon will cook off so these waffles are non-alcoholic!

Yield: 8 servings

Active Time: 15 minutes

Ingredients:

- 2 cups flour
- 1 tablespoon of baking powder
- 1 tablespoon maple syrup
- 1 teaspoons salt
- 2 eggs, lightly whisked
- 1 1/2 cups milk
- 1/3 cup vegetable oil
- 1 tablespoon bourbon

Directions:

1. In a medium bowl, whisk all of the dry ingredients (flour, baking powder, and salt) together.

2. In a separate, small bowl, whisk all of the wet ingredients (the milk, eggs, vegetable oil, maple syrup, and bourbon) together.

3. Slowly add the wet ingredients to the dry, whisking constantly until smooth and lump-free. (If you do have any lumps, use a rubber spatula to press them against the side of the bowl and break them up.)

4. Heat your waffle maker and cook the batter according to your manufacturer's directions.

5. Enjoy these waffles while they are still hot, alone or paired with your favorite toppings.

S'mores Belgian Waffles

The fluffiest waffles, spread with marshmallow fluff and topped with gooey chocolate sauce makes s'mores super easy to make at home – no fire required! While this definitely seems like a dessert, it could pass for breakfast since it's made with waffles.

Yield: 6 servings

Active Time: 15 minutes

Ingredients:

- 2 cups flour
- 1 tablespoon of baking powder
- 4 tablespoons granulated sugar
- 1 teaspoons salt
- 2 eggs separated
- 1 1/2 cups milk

- 1/3 cup vegetable oil
- 1 teaspoon vanilla extract
- 3/4 cup marshmallow fluff
- 1/2 cup chocolate sauce

Directions:

1. In a medium bowl, whisk the egg whites until they form soft peaks. Set aside.

2. In a separate, medium bowl, whisk all of dry ingredients (flour, baking powder, sugar, and salt) together.

3. In another, small bowl, whisk all of the wet ingredients (the milk, vegetable oil, egg yolks, and vanilla) together.

4. Slowly add the wet ingredients to the dry, whisking constantly until smooth and lump-free. (If you do have any lumps, use a rubber spatula to press them against the side of the bowl and break them up.)

5. Gently fold the whipped egg whites into the batter until fully combined.

6. Heat your waffle maker and cook the batter according to your manufacturer's directions.

7. Spread a layer of marshmallow fluff on top of the warm waffles and drizzle with the chocolate sauce. Serve hot!

Espresso Belgian Waffles

Now you can have your coffee and breakfast in one shot! These espresso waffles are full of rich coffee flavor that goes great with maple syrup or whipped cream

Yield: 6 servings

Active Time: 15 minutes

Ingredients:

- 2 cups flour
- 1 tablespoon of baking powder
- 5 tablespoons granulated sugar
- 1 teaspoons salt
- 2 eggs separated
- 1 1/2 cups milk

- 1 tablespoon instant espresso powder
- 1/3 cup vegetable oil
- 1 teaspoon vanilla

Directions:

1. In a small bowl, heat the milk in the microwave and add the espresso powder. Stir to dissolve the espresso and set aside to cool

2. In a medium bowl, whisk the egg whites until they form soft peaks. Set aside.

3. In a separate, medium bowl, whisk all of the dry ingredients (flour, baking powder, sugar, and salt) together.

4. In another, small bowl, whisk all of the wet ingredients (the espresso milk, vegetable oil, egg yolks, and vanilla) together.

5. Slowly add the wet ingredients to the dry, whisking constantly until smooth and lump-free. (If you do have any lumps, use a rubber spatula to press them against the side of the bowl and break them up.)

6. Gently fold the whipped egg whites into the batter until fully combined.

7. Heat your waffle maker and cook the batter according to your manufacturer's directions.

8. Enjoy these waffles while they are still hot, alone or paired with your favorite toppings.

Mocha Belgian Waffles

Chocolate and espresso come together in this perfectly seasoned waffle. If you love mocha lattes and you also love waffles, this is going to be the perfect breakfast for you!

Yield: 6 servings

Active Time: 15 minutes

Ingredients:

- 1 3/4 cups flour
- 1/4 cup cocoa powder
- 1 tablespoon of baking powder
- 5 tablespoons granulated sugar
- 1 teaspoons salt
- 2 eggs separated
- 1 1/2 cups milk
- 1 tablespoon instant espresso powder
- 1/3 cup vegetable oil
- 2 teaspoons vanilla

Directions:

1. In a small bowl, heat the milk in the microwave and add the espresso powder. Stir to dissolve the espresso and set aside to cool

2. In a medium bowl, whisk the egg whites until they form soft peaks. Set aside.

3. In a separate, medium bowl, whisk all of dry ingredients (flour, baking powder, cocoa powder, sugar, and salt) together.

4. In another, small bowl, whisk all of the wet ingredients (the espresso milk, vegetable oil, egg yolks, and vanilla) together.

5. Slowly add the wet ingredients to the dry, whisking constantly until smooth and lump-free. (If you do have any

lumps, use a rubber spatula to press them against the side of the bowl and break them up.)

6. Gently fold the whipped egg whites into the batter until fully combined.

7. Heat your waffle maker and cook the batter according to your manufacturer's directions.

8. Top with chocolate sauce or eat plain.

Oreo Waffles

These are great for any kids (and adults) who love cookies and cream. Super easy to make, you will be enjoying these waffles in no time and will love making them for breakfast any day of the week!

Yield: 8 servings

Active Time: 15 minutes

Ingredients:

- 1 3/4 cups flour
- 1/2 cup Oreo crumbs
- 1 tablespoon of baking powder
- 4 tablespoons granulated sugar
- 1 teaspoons salt

- 2 eggs, lightly whisked
- 1 1/2 cups milk
- 1/3 cup vegetable oil
- 1 teaspoon vanilla extract

Directions:

1. In a medium bowl, whisk all of the dry ingredients (flour, Oreo crumbs, baking powder, sugar and salt) together.

2. In a separate, small bowl, whisk all of the wet ingredients (the milk, eggs, vegetable oil, and vanilla) together.

3. Slowly add the wet ingredients to the dry, whisking constantly until smooth and lump-free. (If you do have any lumps, use a rubber spatula to press them against the side of the bowl and break them up.)

4. Heat your waffle maker and cook the batter according to your manufacturer's directions.

5. Enjoy these waffles while they are still hot, alone or paired with your favorite toppings.

Cinnamon-Sugar Churro Belgian Waffles

Churros are such a delicious dessert that they must make a good waffle too, right? That's right! These easy-to-make churro waffles are perfect for dessert, a snack, or breakfast. As they are cut into nice strips, they are the perfect finger food!

Yield: 8 servings

Active Time: 15 minutes

Ingredients:

- 2 cups flour
- 1 teaspoon cinnamon
- 1 tablespoon of baking powder
- 4 tablespoons granulated sugar
- 1 teaspoons salt
- 2 eggs, lightly whisked
- 1 1/2 cups milk
- 1/3 cup vegetable oil
- 1 teaspoon vanilla extract
- 1/4 cup sugar
- 1 tablespoon cinnamon

Directions:

1. In a small bowl, add the 1 tablespoon of cinnamon and 1/4 cup sugar. Set aside.

2. In a medium bowl, whisk the flour, baking powder, 1 teaspoon cinnamon, 4 tablespoons sugar, and salt together.

3. In a separate, small bowl, whisk all of the wet ingredients (the milk, eggs, vegetable oil, and vanilla) together.

4. Slowly add the wet ingredients to the dry, whisking constantly until smooth and lump-free. (If you do have any lumps, use a rubber spatula to press them against the side of the bowl and break them up.)

5. Heat your waffle maker and cook the batter according to your manufacturer's directions.

6. When the waffles are cooked, cut them into strips following the lines of the waffle.

7. Dip the strips into the cinnamon and sugar mix and serve hot with some chocolate sauce for dipping.

Pumpkin Chocolate Chip Belgian Waffles

Pumpkin and chocolate go so well together and these pumpkin chocolate chip waffles are no exception. Full of melty chocolate chips and mouth watering pumpkin flavor, they are sure to be a hit!

Yield: 8 Servings

Active Time: 15 minutes

Ingredients:

- 3/4 cup chocolate chips
- 1/2 cup coconut oil
- 1/2 cup brown sugar
- 1/4 cup white sugar
- 1 1/2 cups pumpkin puree
- 2 separated eggs
- 1/2 cup whole milk
- 3 teaspoons vanilla extract
- 1 1/2 Tablespoons pumpkin spice
- 1 1/2 cups flour
- 3 teaspoons baking powder
- 1/2 teaspoon salt

Directions:

1. Using a hand blender, whip the egg whites to medium soft peaks. Then, set aside for now

2. In a large bowl, mix the coconut oil, milk, sugars, pumpkin puree, and yolks. Whisk until smooth.

3. Add the pumpkin spice and vanilla extract to the bowl with the pumpkin and mix together.

4. Add the dry ingredients to the bowl and whisk until smooth.

5. Gently add the egg whites into the batter. Mix until combined but don't beat the batter too hard- you want it to stay nice and fluffy

6. Fold the chocolate chips into the batter

7. Preheat your waffle iron then pour the batter in and close to cook.

8. Once the waffles are done, remove from the waffle iron and serve!

30299784R00047

Made in the USA
Middletown, DE
24 December 2018